I Wonder Why

Caterpillars Eat So Much

and Other Questions About Life Cycles

Belinda Weber

KINGFISHER

BOSTON

KINGFISHER

a Houghton Mifflin
    Company imprint
222 Berkeley Street
Boston, Massachusetts 02116
www.houghtonmifflinbooks.com

First published in 2006
10 9 8 7 6 5 4 3 2
2TR/1106/SHE/RNB(RNB)/126.6MA/F

LIBRARY OF CONGRESS CATALOGING-IN-PUBLICATION DATA
Weber, Belinda.
I wonder why caterpillars eat so much and other
questions about life cycles/Belinda Weber.—1st ed.
  p. cm.
Includes index.
1. Life cycles (Biology)—Juvenile literature. I. Title.
QH501.W43 2006
571.8—dc22   2005031716

ISBN-10: 0-7534-6030-0
ISBN-13: 978-07534-6030-6

Editors: Simon Holland, Russell McLean,
    Hannah Wilson
Coordinating editor: Caitlin Doyle
Senior art editor and visualizer: Dominic Zwemmer
Consultant: David Burnie
DTP manager: Nicky Studdart
DTP operator: Claire Cessford
Production controller: Lindsey Scott
Illustrations: Martin Camm 4–5, 8–9, 12–13,
14–15, 20–21, 24–25, 28–29; Michael Langham
Rowe 6–7, 10–11, 16–17, 18–19, 22–23, 26–27,
30–31; Peter Wilks (SGA) all cartoons

Printed in Taiwan

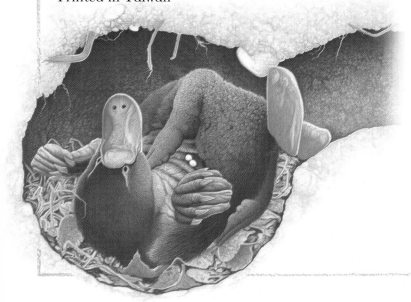

CONTENTS

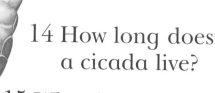
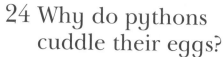

egg is laid by
butterfly

1

? What is a life cycle?

A life cycle is a series
of changes that happens
to every living thing. It starts
from the moment that an egg is
fertilized and continues until death.
Not all life cycles are the same, but
they often follow the same type of pattern.

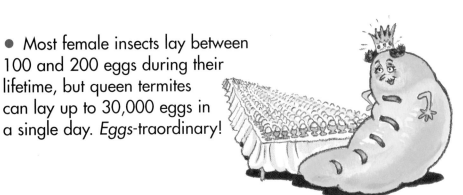

● The caterpillar of the
monarch butterfly eats
a plant called milkweed.
If it eats enough, it can
get around 2,000 times
heavier in just two weeks!

● Most female insects lay between
100 and 200 eggs during their
lifetime, but queen termites
can lay up to 30,000 eggs in
a single day. *Eggs*-traordinary!

What is the first step in a life cycle?

The first step in a life cycle is
usually when an egg is fertilized.
Two adults of the same species
(type) mate and produce young.
In butterflies, the young start
out as tiny eggs. A caterpillar
grows inside of each egg until
it is ready to hatch.

caterpillar hatches
from egg

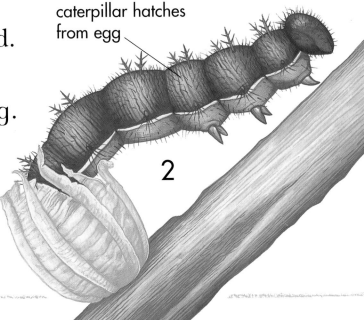

2

3

pupa forms
around caterpillar

Why do caterpillars eat so much?

When a caterpillar hatches, it eats leaves until it is as big as it can grow. Then it makes a pupa, or hard case, around its body. The caterpillar changes into a butterfly inside of this case.

● Each life cycle ends when the adult creature dies. But if the creature leaves young behind, a new cycle of life begins.

How does a butterfly get out?

The pupa splits open so that the butterfly can crawl out. It pumps blood into its crumpled wings to open them up, then it stays in the sun until they are dry. Then the adult butterfly flies off to find a mate and start a new life cycle.

4

pupa splits open

5

butterfly emerges from pupa

Do all living things reproduce?

Yes, living things produce young in order to make sure that their species survives. A female pig can have up to 12 babies at a time. When the piglets have grown into adults, they will have babies of their own.

● Bacteria can split apart and make millions of young in just a few hours. Some bacteria are harmless, but others can cause infections in people.

Why do animals have two parents?

Most animals, including mammals and birds, have two parents—a male and a female. The parents produce a totally new individual because they both pass on their genes to their baby. Genes control the way that an animal looks.

● Mayflies live life in the fast lane! Some only live for a few hours as adults and must find a mate before they die.

Which living thing divides into two?

Amoebas are shapeless blobs that live in the water. They are tiny living things that are only made up of one cell (cells are the building blocks that make up every living thing). Like bacteria, amoebas reproduce by splitting themselves into two.

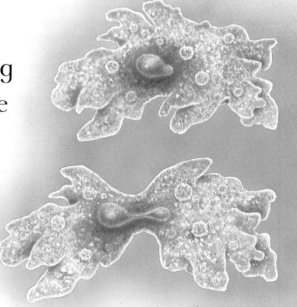

amoeba splitting into two

● Mice and other rodents breed very quickly. A pair of house mice can produce 14 litters, or sets, of babies in just one year!

Why do turtles have lots of babies?

Some animals have lots of babies to make sure that at least some of them survive. Hundreds of baby turtles hatch at the same time and head toward the sea. Gulls and lizards try to eat them, but because there are so many turtles, a large number will survive.

● When a mother shrew moves, her babies form a long line by holding onto each other's tails with their teeth!

Do any animals only have one baby?

Yes, orangutans only have one baby at a time. This gives the mother more time to feed and take care of the baby and keep it safe. The baby grows slowly but learns how to survive. This increases the chances of it becoming an adult.

gull

lizard

hatching
turtle

bee-eaters

Do moms and dads get help?

Sometimes, they do. Bee-eaters are birds that eat bees and other insects. Bee-eater parents can't carry enough food to feed all of their babies, so their older children help them.

● Humans usually give birth to one child at a time but sometimes more. In 1997 an American woman gave birth to seven babies at once!

Do plants have babies?

Most plants produce seeds that grow into new plants. Flowering plants produce seeds when they are fertilized. Insects, such as bees, help fertilize plants by carrying pollen from one flower to another. The fertilized plant then produces its seeds.

• Seeds may be small, but they contain all the building blocks that a plant needs in order to grow. A tiny acorn can grow into an oak tree that is more than 130 feet tall!

• Bees like to eat the dustlike pollen that is made by flowers. As a bee flies around, it spreads pollen from flower to flower and fertilizes the plants.

pollen

foxglove flower (cut open)

Why are seeds spread?

Seeds need to be spread away from a plant so that they can have enough space to grow. When an animal eats a fruit, the tough seeds pass out of the animal in its droppings. The droppings help the seed grow into a new plant.

monkey eating a fruit

● Some seeds have spiky or sticky cases. These get stuck in an animal's fur and are carried to new places when the animal moves around.

strawberry plant

runner

Which plant "runs"?

Some plants can make new plants by sending out shoots. Strawberries, for example, produce shoots, called runners, without being fertilized. They also make flowers that are fertilized and form seeds.

● Puffballs use the wind to carry away their spores, which are similar to seeds. When the puffball is ripe, it releases the spores into the air.

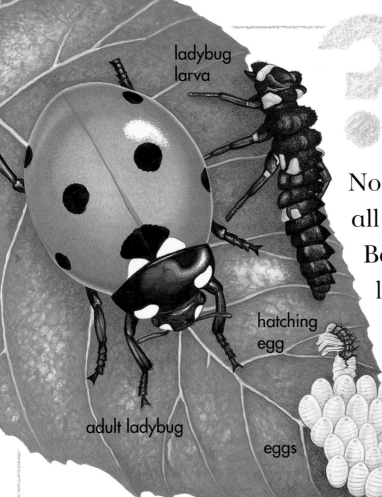

ladybug larva

hatching egg

adult ladybug

eggs

Do animals make seeds?

No, animals make babies. But not all babies look like their parents. Baby insects, such as ladybug larvae (the developing young), often look very different from the adults. But as they grow, they change. Eventually, they will mate and have babies of their own.

Why do birds lay eggs?

Birds have to fly in order to find food, so they cannot carry heavy babies inside of them. By laying babies inside of eggs, a female bird can have more babies, and each one has a safe place in which to develop.

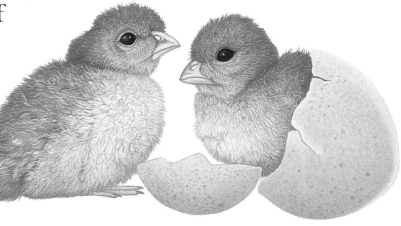

● Tadpoles look very different to adult frogs. But in just a few weeks they grow legs and start to look like their parents.

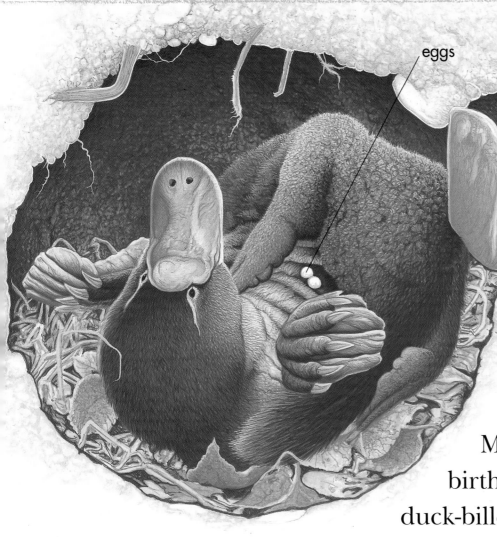

eggs

underground nest of female duck-billed platypus

Do any mammals lay eggs?

Most mammals give birth to live young, but the duck-billed platypus lays eggs. The female platypus lays two or three small eggs, and the eggs hatch after around ten days. The mother feeds the babies with milk for up to five months.

● The duck-billed platypus is an amazing builder. It digs tunnels in riverbanks to make safe nests. The entrances to the tunnels are often underwater.

● The ostrich lays the heaviest egg of any bird. Each egg can weigh up to three pounds!

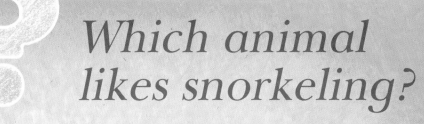

Which animal likes snorkeling?

Mosquitoes lay their eggs in still water. When the young hatch, they need to breathe air, so they poke a special tube out through the surface of the water. This acts like a snorkel and lets them breathe in air.

breathing tube

mosquito larva underwater

● Some types of wood-boring beetles' larvae take 40 years to develop from eggs into adults!

How long does a cicada live?

A cicada spends most of its life underground, feeding on the sap (juice) of plants. It stays like this for up to 17 years. It then crawls up a tree, sheds its skin one last time, and becomes an adult. The adult cicada only lives for a few weeks.

old skin

emerging cicada

Why does a glowworm glow?

A glowworm is a beetle that makes a light in its body. The female glowworm has a special organ in her abdomen (lower body) that gives off light. The female glows to signal to a male that she is nearby and ready to mate.

● Unlike most insects, female earwigs guard their eggs from predators until they hatch.

● If you threaten an elephant hawk moth caterpillar, it will suck in air and inflate its head to make itself look too big to eat!

Why do insects hide their eggs?

Insects hide their eggs to stop other animals from eating them. Cabbage butterflies lay their eggs on the underside of cabbage leaves. This hides the eggs and also provides fresh leaves for the young to eat.

What do spiders keep in sacs?

Many spiders wrap up their eggs in a silk sac and carry this sac around to keep the eggs safe. Green lynx spiders tie their egg sac to a cactus leaf with long strings of silk.

● Some spiders cover their egg sacs with mud or dried plants. This disguises them from hungry predators.

What do baby spiders look like?

Spiderlings, or baby spiders, look like tiny adult spiders. Some species of garden spiders stay together for a few days after they hatch and form a tightly packed ball. If they are threatened, the ball splits open, and the spiderlings run away.

Why do spiders split open?

Like all invertebrates (animals without backbones), spiders have a tough case around their body, like a suit of armor. When the spider grows, the case splits open, and the bigger spider crawls out. Its skin takes a few hours to harden.

● The female garden spider lays her eggs very quickly. She can lay more than 1,000 eggs in less than ten minutes.

Why do spiders go ballooning?

● Wolf spiderlings hitch a ride on their mother's back. All the babies trail silk threads, and if they fall off, they climb back up along their thread.

Many spiders are so tiny that they cannot travel very far on their legs. But they can hitch a ride on the wind. They spin threads and dangle from them in the air. This is called ballooning.

Do fish lay eggs?

Yes, most fish lay thousands and thousands of eggs. They have to lay so many eggs because very few will survive to become adults and find their own mates. The female lays her eggs in the water, and the male fertilizes them.

male porcupine fish

eggs

female porcupine fish

● Whale sharks are the world's biggest fish, but they only eat tiny creatures called plankton. They slurp up millions in each mouthful.

Which fish swallows its babies?

Mouthbreeders, such as cichlids, are fish that carry their eggs in their mouths. Even after they hatch, the adult will scoop the little fish back into the safety of its mouth at the first sign of danger.

• Male damselfish protect their territory during the mating season and will fight off anything that gets too close— even human divers!

Why do fish dance?

Some fish dance or change color in order to attract a mate. Male sticklebacks become more colorful when they are ready to breed. They build a nest in the weeds and tempt a female to lay her eggs in it by doing a special zigzag dance.

male stickleback

• Baby fish and fish eggs are eaten by lots of other sea animals. In order to stay safe, many rise to the ocean's surface and feed among the plants that grow there.

When do sea horses pop?

A female sea horse lays her eggs in a special pouch on the front of the male. There, the eggs develop into miniature sea horses. When they are ready to hatch, the young pop out of their father's pouch.

● The oldest fish on record was a North American lake sturgeon. It died at the age of 152!

What is a mermaid's purse?

A mermaid's purse is the tough outer casing of a cat shark's egg. The female lays around 20 eggs, which she attaches to seaweed. After around nine months a shark pup breaks free from each egg.

shark pup

Do all sharks lay eggs?

No, thresher sharks give birth to
around four live young at a time.
The female keeps the eggs inside
of her until they hatch. The first
ones out of the eggs often
eat their brothers
and sisters.

● In warm waters
swell shark eggs develop
in around seven months.
In colder waters it can
take ten months.

baby thresher
shark being born

Where do baby sharks live?

Sharks are under threat from larger
predators when they are babies.
Lemon sharks are born in shallow
lagoons. They live there safely for
around seven or eight years, teaming up
with other young of around the same size.

Which eggs wobble?

Frogs lay thousands of jellylike eggs that stick together to form a huge, wobbly mass. A tiny baby frog, called a tadpole, develops inside of each egg. Toads also lay eggs. Their eggs form a long, sticky string that is up to three feet in length.

frogs' eggs

tadpoles

● Red-eyed tree frogs start their lives with a splash. The female lays her eggs on leaves above pools of water. When the eggs hatch, the tadpoles drop into the pools. They climb back up the trees when they are adults.

How do tadpoles breathe?

When they first hatch from their eggs, tadpoles have long tails for swimming and gills to allow them to breathe underwater. Gills are frilly flaps of skin on the sides of their heads. The tadpoles use their gills to take a gas called oxygen from the water.

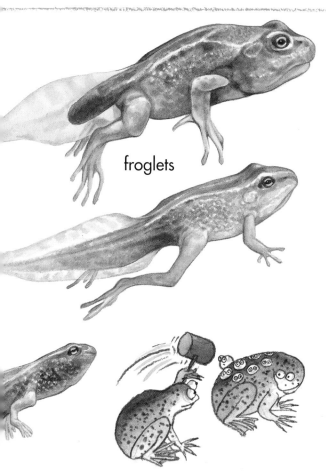

froglets

Why do tadpoles grow legs?

As they become older, tadpoles change. After a few weeks they grow back legs, then front legs. Their tail and gills shrink back into their bodies, and they develop lungs to breathe air. The small froglets are now ready to start life on land.

● When a female Surinam toad lays her eggs, the male squishes them into the spongy skin on her back.

● Mouthbreeder frog tadpoles live in their father's mouth for the first weeks of their lives. Then he spits them out!

Why are frogs so noisy?

Many frogs and toads make loud calls in order to attract a mate. Bullfrogs have a special pouch under their chins. They inflate this pouch like a balloon to make their call really loud. It can be heard from one mile away!

Why do pythons cuddle their eggs?

Most reptiles lay eggs and then leave them to hatch on their own. But some take care of their eggs, keeping them warm and safe from predators. The green tree python coils around her eggs. By keeping the eggs warm, she helps the unborn babies develop quicker.

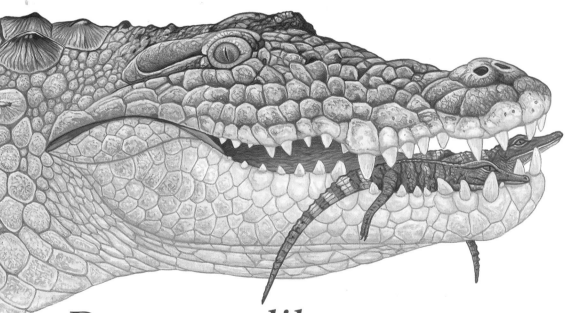

Do crocodiles eat their babies?

A baby crocodile only weighs nine ounces when it hatches, but its mother weighs around 2,000 times that much! Although it looks as if she is eating her babies, she is actually carrying them carefully from their nest to the water.

● Baby rattlesnakes can't make the warning rattle sound. The snake must shed its skin several times before the rattle builds up at the end of its tail.

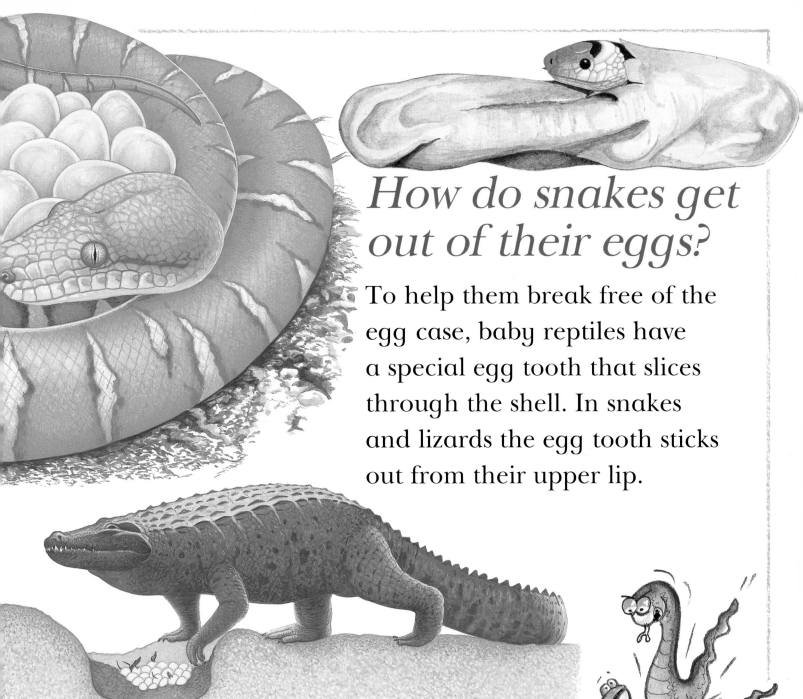

How do snakes get out of their eggs?

To help them break free of the egg case, baby reptiles have a special egg tooth that slices through the shell. In snakes and lizards the egg tooth sticks out from their upper lip.

When do eggs yelp?

Crocodiles bury their eggs in order to keep them warm. But the baby crocodiles cannot dig themselves out. So just before they are ready to hatch, they yelp, grunt, and croak inside the eggs. The mother hears her babies and digs them out of the nest.

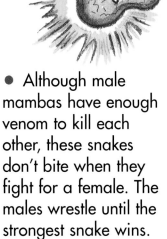

● Although male mambas have enough venom to kill each other, these snakes don't bite when they fight for a female. The males wrestle until the strongest snake wins.

Why do cranes dance?

Birds find a mate by putting on a courtship display. Male cranes strut around and dance in front of their chosen female, bowing down low, then leaping high up into the air.

● Hornbills make nests inside of holes in trees. The female seals herself inside and lays her eggs. Her mate brings her food.

Which bird is a great weaver?

Birds build nests to provide a safe home for their young. The male weaver from Africa weaves grasses into a ball-shaped nest that hangs down from a tree. If a female likes the nest, she will mate with the male.

● Cuckoos are very lazy parents. They lay their eggs in other birds' nests. The young cuckoo kills any other chicks that hatch and demands all the food for itself!

How do penguins' eggs stay warm?

Emperor penguins breed in the frozen lands of Antarctica. The males carry the egg on their feet in order to keep it warm. They have a special fold of skin under their bellies that helps keep the egg or chick warm.

Who takes care of baby birds?

Usually both parents bring food to their chicks. Wandering albatross only lay one large egg, which takes around 80 days to hatch. Albatross eat fish, and the parents take turns taking care of the egg and hunting far out at sea.

Which newborn babies can run fast?

Foals (baby horses) can stand up around ten minutes after they are born. They can run fast in just a few hours. Like most mammals, foals grow inside their mothers for a long time, so they are well developed when they are born.

● Female pigs have 12 teats for feeding milk to their young. They can feed a dozen piglets at a time!

Why do kangaroos have pouches?

Kangaroos give birth when their babies are still underdeveloped. The tiny baby is only as long as your thumb. It crawls into its mother's pouch for warmth and safety, as well as for food. The mother produces milk in her pouch to feed her baby.

Are tigers good dads?

Male tigers are solitary animals, which means that they like to live alone. They never see or take care of their cubs. They only meet females when they want to mate.

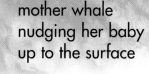

mother whale nudging her baby up to the surface

Are any mammals born underwater?

Whales and dolphins give birth to their young in the sea. Because they are mammals, they need to breathe air, so the mother or her sisters gently nudge the baby up to the surface of the water for its first breath.

● Dayak fruit bats from Borneo are unusual because the males can produce milk. They are the only male mammals that are able to do this.

Why do elephant seals fight?

Male elephant seals fight in order to show who is the strongest. The male who wins the most fights gets the largest territory and will mate with more females.

● Male bighorn sheep crash their horns together to see who is the strongest.

jackals

What happens to old animals?

Most animals don't get to be very old in the wild. They may not be fit enough to keep up with the herd, or they may be picked off by predators. When they die, their bodies provide food for other animals such as jackals.

zebra

Why do animals play?

Baby animals learn by playing. When lion cubs chase their mother's twitching tail, they learn the skills they will need to hunt. By creeping through the long grasses, the cubs learn how to stalk prey.

● Male rhinos leave smelly piles of dung to show females where they are!

Which animals live the longest?

Humans live the longest of all mammals because we have better access to food, water, and shelter than other mammals. In Europe and the U.S. most men live to be around 75 and women to 80. But the oldest animal of all time was not a mammal, but a 188-year-old tortoise!

Index

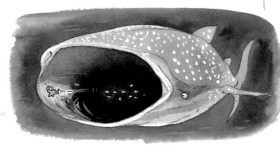